FAMOUS FONTS

A Coloring Book of Typefaces

David Sorkin

ISBN 978-1-5306-1140-9

Arial

Arial was developed for Monotype in 1982, as a substitute for Helvetica. It is one of the core fonts included with Microsoft Windows, and is among the most widely used fonts for that reason.

Baskerville

ABCD

abcdefg

Baskerville was designed by John Baskerville in 1757. Baskerville was illiterate, but was very interested in calligraphy.

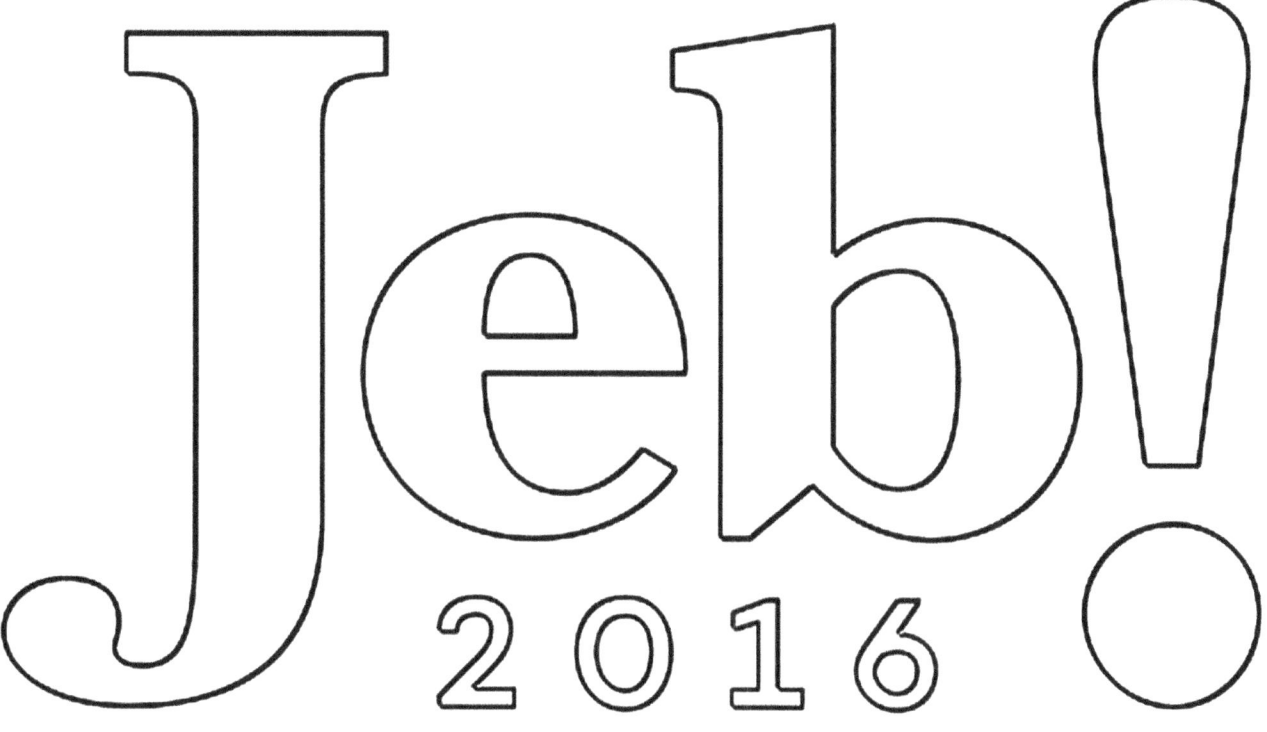

The logo for Jeb Bush's ill-fated 2016 presidential campaign used Baskerville as its primary typeface.

Bauhaus

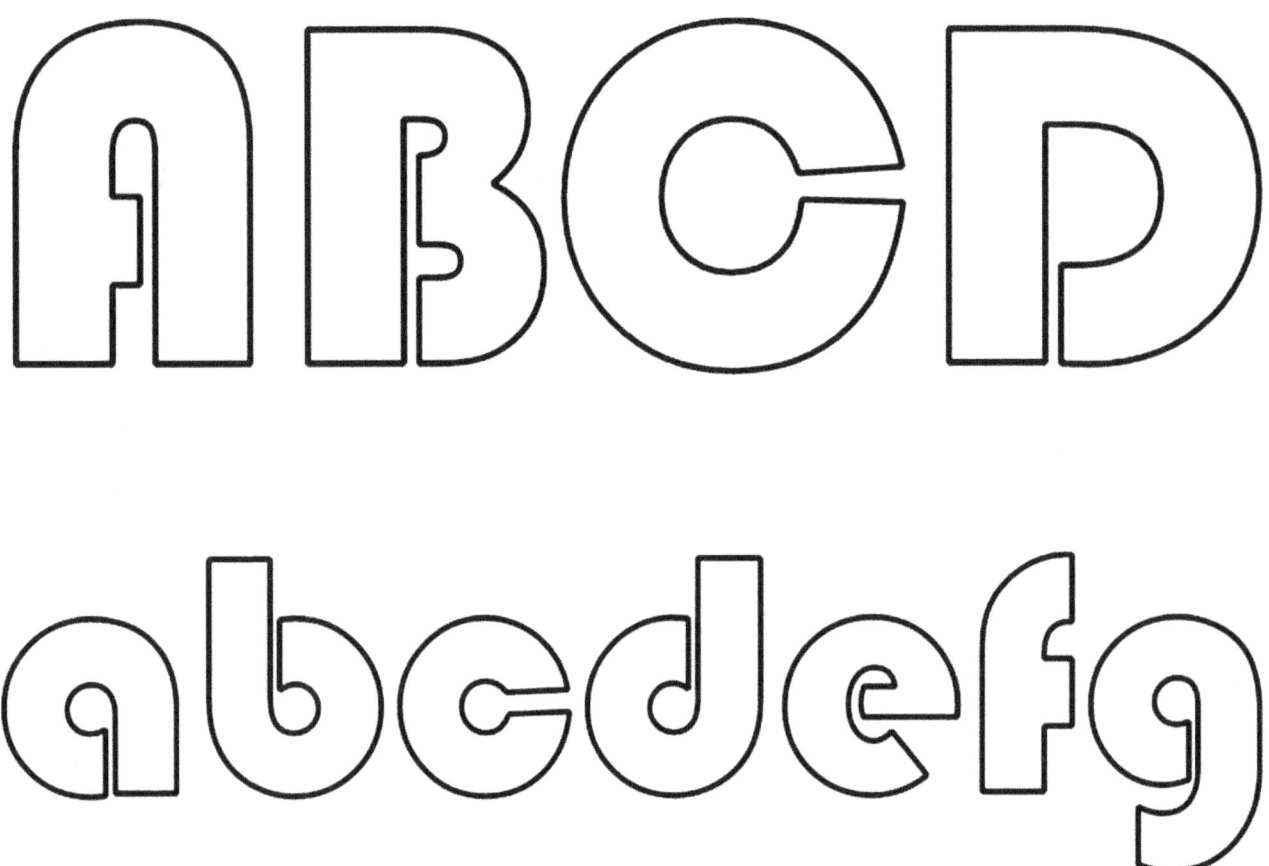

Bauhaus was based upon the 1920s Universal Typeface designs of Herbert Bayer, a member of the Bauhaus movement.

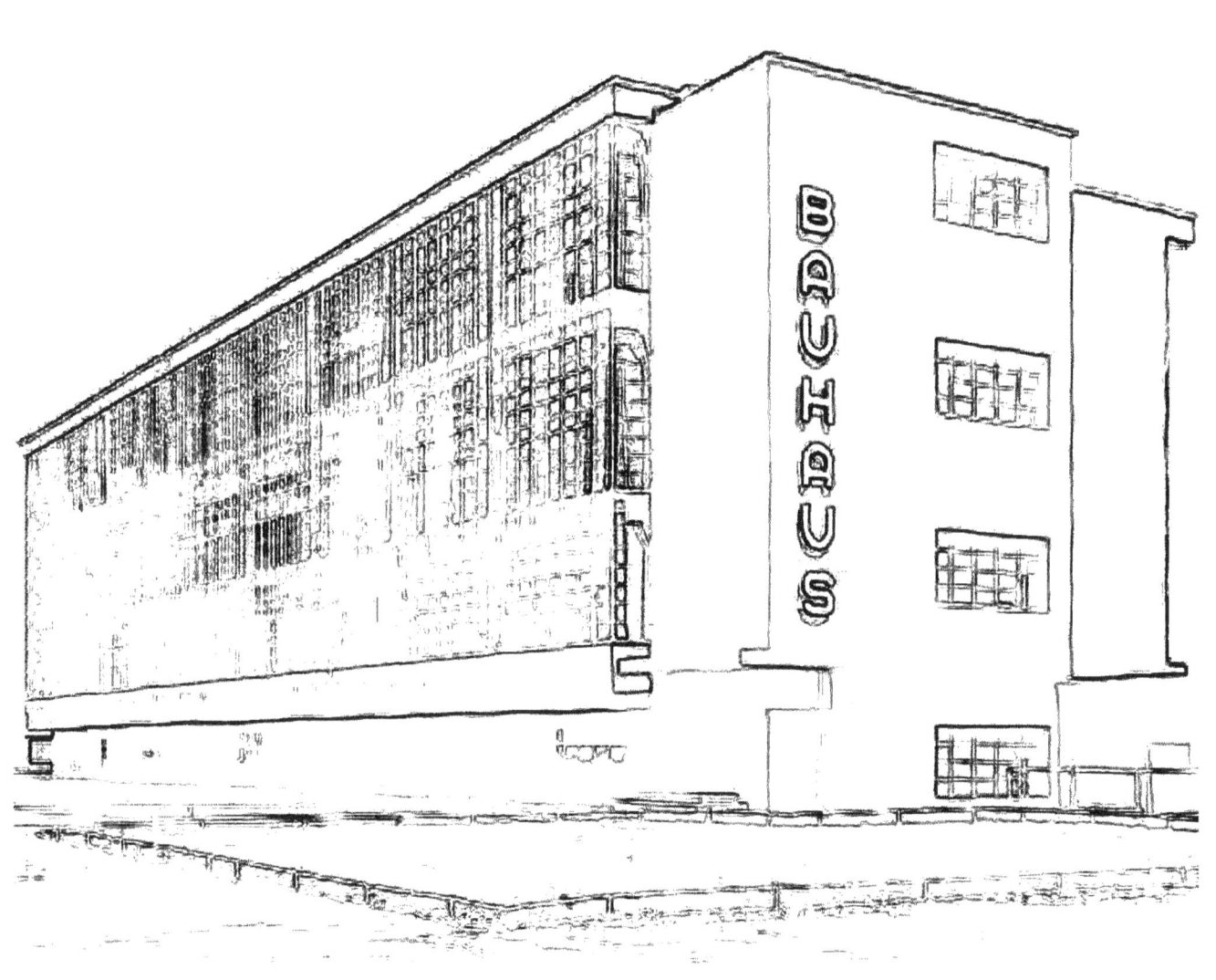

Ludwig Mies van der Rohe led the
Bauhaus school in Dessau, Germany,
in the early 1930s.

Bodoni

Eighteenth century type designer Giambattista Bodoni was inspired by John Baskerville. A wide variety of Bodoni-style typefaces are now available.

Nirvana's logo is set in
Bodoni Poster Compressed.

Caslon

ABCD
abcdefg

Caslon was designed by William Caslon I in about 1730.

IN CONGRESS, JULY 4, 1776.

A DECLARATION

BY THE REPRESENTATIVES OF THE

UNITED STATES OF AMERICA,

IN GENERAL CONGRESS ASSEMBLED.

WHEN in the Course of human Events, it becomes neceſſary for one People to diſſolve the Political Bands which have connected them with another, and to aſſume among the Powers of the Earth, the ſeparate and equal Station to which the Laws of Nature and of Nature's God entitle them, a decent Reſpect to the Opinions of Mankind requires that they ſhould declare the cauſes which impel them to the Separation.

We hold theſe Truths to be ſelf-evident, that all Men are created equal, that they are endowed by their Creator with certain unalienable Rights, that among theſe are Life, Liberty, and the Purſuit of Happineſs——That to ſecure theſe Rights, Governments are inſtituted among Men, deriving their juſt Powers from the Conſent of the Governed, that whenever any Form of Government becomes deſtructive of theſe Ends, it is the Right of the People to alter or to aboliſh it, and to inſtitute new Government, laying its Foundation on ſuch Principles, and organizing its Powers in ſuch Form, as to them ſhall ſeem moſt likely to effect their Safety and Happineſs. Prudence, indeed, will dictate that Governments long eſtabliſhed ſhould not be changed for light and tranſient Cauſes; and accordingly all Experience hath ſhewn, that Mankind are more diſpoſed to ſuffer, while Evils are ſufferable, than to right themſelves by aboliſhing the Forms to which they are accuſtomed. But when a long Train of Abuſes and Uſurpations, purſuing invariably the ſame Object, evinces a Deſign to reduce them under abſolute Deſpotiſm, it is their Right, it is their Duty, to throw off ſuch Government, and to provide new Guards for their future Security. Such has been the patient Sufferance of theſe Colonies; and ſuch is now the Neceſſity which conſtrains them to alter their former Syſtems of Government. The Hiſtory of the preſent King of Great-Britain is a Hiſtory of repeated Injuries and Uſurpations, all having in direct Object the Eſtabliſhment of an abſolute Tyranny over theſe States. To prove this, let Facts be ſubmitted to a candid World.

He has refuſed his Aſſent to Laws, the moſt wholeſome and neceſſary for the public Good.

He has forbidden his Governors to paſs Laws of immediate and preſſing Importance, unleſs ſuſpended in their Operation till his Aſſent ſhould be obtained; and when ſo ſuſpended, he has utterly neglected to attend to them.

He has refuſed to paſs other Laws for the Accommodation of large Diſtricts of People, unleſs thoſe People would relinquiſh the Right of Repreſentation in the Legiſlature, a Right ineſtimable to them, and formidable to Tyrants only.

He has called together Legiſlative Bodies at Places unuſual, uncomfortable, and diſtant from the Depoſitory of their public Records, for the ſole Purpoſe of fatiguing them into Compliance with his Meaſures.

He has diſſolved Repreſentative Houſes repeatedly, for oppoſing with manly Firmneſs his Invaſions on the Rights of the People.

He has refuſed for a long Time, after ſuch Diſſolutions, to cauſe others to be elected; whereby the Legiſlative Powers, incapable of Annihilation, have returned to the People at large for their exerciſe; the State remaining in the mean time expoſed to all the Dangers of Invaſion from without, and Convulſions within.

He has endeavoured to prevent the Population of theſe States; for that Purpoſe obſtructing the Laws for Naturalization of Foreigners; refuſing to paſs others to encourage their Migrations hither, and raiſing the Conditions of new Appropriations of Lands.

He has obſtructed the Adminiſtration of Juſtice, by refuſing his Aſſent to Laws for eſtabliſhing Judiciary Powers.

He has made Judges dependent on his Will alone, for the Tenure of their Offices, and the Amount and Payment of their Salaries.

He has erected a Multitude of new Offices, and ſent hither Swarms of Officers to harraſs our People, and eat out their Subſtance.

He has kept among us, in Times of Peace, Standing Armies, without the conſent of our Legiſlatures.

He has affected to render the Military independent of and ſuperior to the Civil Power.

He has combined with others to ſubject us to a Juriſdiction foreign to our Conſtitution, and unacknowledged by our Laws; giving his Aſſent to their Acts of pretended Legiſlation:

For quartering large Bodies of Armed Troops among us:

For protecting them, by a mock Trial, from Puniſhment for any Murders which they ſhould commit on the Inhabitants of theſe States:

For cutting off our Trade with all Parts of the World:

For impoſing Taxes on us without our Conſent:

For depriving us, in many Caſes, of the Benefits of Trial by Jury:

For tranſporting us beyond Seas to be tried for pretended Offences:

For aboliſhing the free Syſtem of Engliſh Laws in a neighbouring Province, eſtabliſhing therein an arbitrary Government, and enlarging its Boundaries, ſo as to render it at once an Example and fit Inſtrument for introducing the ſame abſolute Rule into theſe Colonies:

For taking away our Charters, aboliſhing our moſt valuable Laws, and altering fundamentally the Forms of our Governments:

For ſuſpending our own Legiſlatures, and declaring themſelves inveſted with Power to legiſlate for us in all Caſes whatſoever.

He has abdicated Government here, by declaring us out of his Protection and waging War againſt us.

He has plundered our Seas, ravaged our Coaſts, burnt our Towns, and deſtroyed the Lives of our People.

He is, at this Time, tranſporting large Armies of foreign Mercenaries to compleat the Works of Death, Deſolation, and Tyranny, already begun with circumſtances of Cruelty and Perfidy, ſcarcely paralleled in the moſt barbarous Ages, and totally unworthy the Head of a civilized Nation.

He has conſtrained our fellow Citizens taken Captive on the high Seas to bear Arms againſt their Country, to become the Executioners of their Friends and Brethren, or to fall themſelves by their Hands.

He has excited domeſtic Inſurrections amongſt us, and has endeavoured to bring on the Inhabitants of our Frontiers, the mercileſs Indian Savages, whoſe known Rule of Warfare, is an undiſtinguiſhed Deſtruction, of all Ages, Sexes and Conditions.

In every ſtage of theſe Oppreſſions we have Petitioned for Redreſs in the moſt humble Terms: Our repeated Petitions have been anſwered only by repeated Injury. A Prince, whoſe Character is thus marked by every act which may define a Tyrant, is unfit to be the Ruler of a free People.

Nor have we been wanting in Attentions to our Britiſh Brethren. We have warned them from Time to Time of Attempts by their Legiſlature to extend an unwarrantable Juriſdiction over us. We have reminded them of the Circumſtances of our Emigration and Settlement here. We have appealed to their native Juſtice and Magnanimity, and we have conjured them by the Ties of our common Kindred to diſavow theſe Uſurpations, which, would inevitably interrupt our Connections and Correſpondence. They too have been deaf to the Voice of Juſtice and of Conſanguinity. We muſt, therefore, acquieſce in the Neceſſity, which denounces our Separation, and hold them, as we hold the reſt of Mankind, Enemies in War, in Peace, Friends.

We, therefore, the Repreſentatives of the UNITED STATES OF AMERICA, in GENERAL CONGRESS, Aſſembled, appealing to the Supreme Judge of the World for the Rectitude of our Intentions, do, in the Name, and by Authority of the good People of theſe Colonies, ſolemnly Publiſh and Declare, That theſe United Colonies are, and of Right ought to be, FREE AND INDEPENDENT STATES; that they are abſolved from all Allegiance to the Britiſh Crown, and that all political Connection between them and the State of Great-Britain, is and ought to be totally diſſolved; and that as FREE AND INDEPENDENT STATES, they have full Power to levy War, conclude Peace, contract Alliances, eſtabliſh Commerce, and to do all other Acts and Things which INDEPENDENT STATES may of right do. And for the ſupport of this Declaration, with a firm Reliance on the Protection of divine Providence, we mutually pledge to each other our Lives, our Fortunes, and our ſacred Honor.

Signed by ORDER and in BEHALF of the CONGRESS,

JOHN HANCOCK, PRESIDENT.

ATTEST.
CHARLES THOMSON, SECRETARY.

PHILADELPHIA: PRINTED BY JOHN DUNLAP.

Benjamin Franklin was a fan of Caslon.

Century Gothic

Century Gothic was released by Monotype Imaging in 1991. It was influenced by geometric typefaces of the 1920s and 1930s, including Futura and Twentieth Century.

Century Schoolbook

ABCD

abcdefg

Century Schoolbook was designed by Morris Fuller Benton in 1919 for the American Type Founders. It is based upon Century Roman, created by Benton's father, L. B. Benton, in 1894.

Clarendon

ABCD

abcdefg

Clarendon was created by Robert Besley in about 1842. It was especially popular for posters printed with wood type.

Comic Sans MS

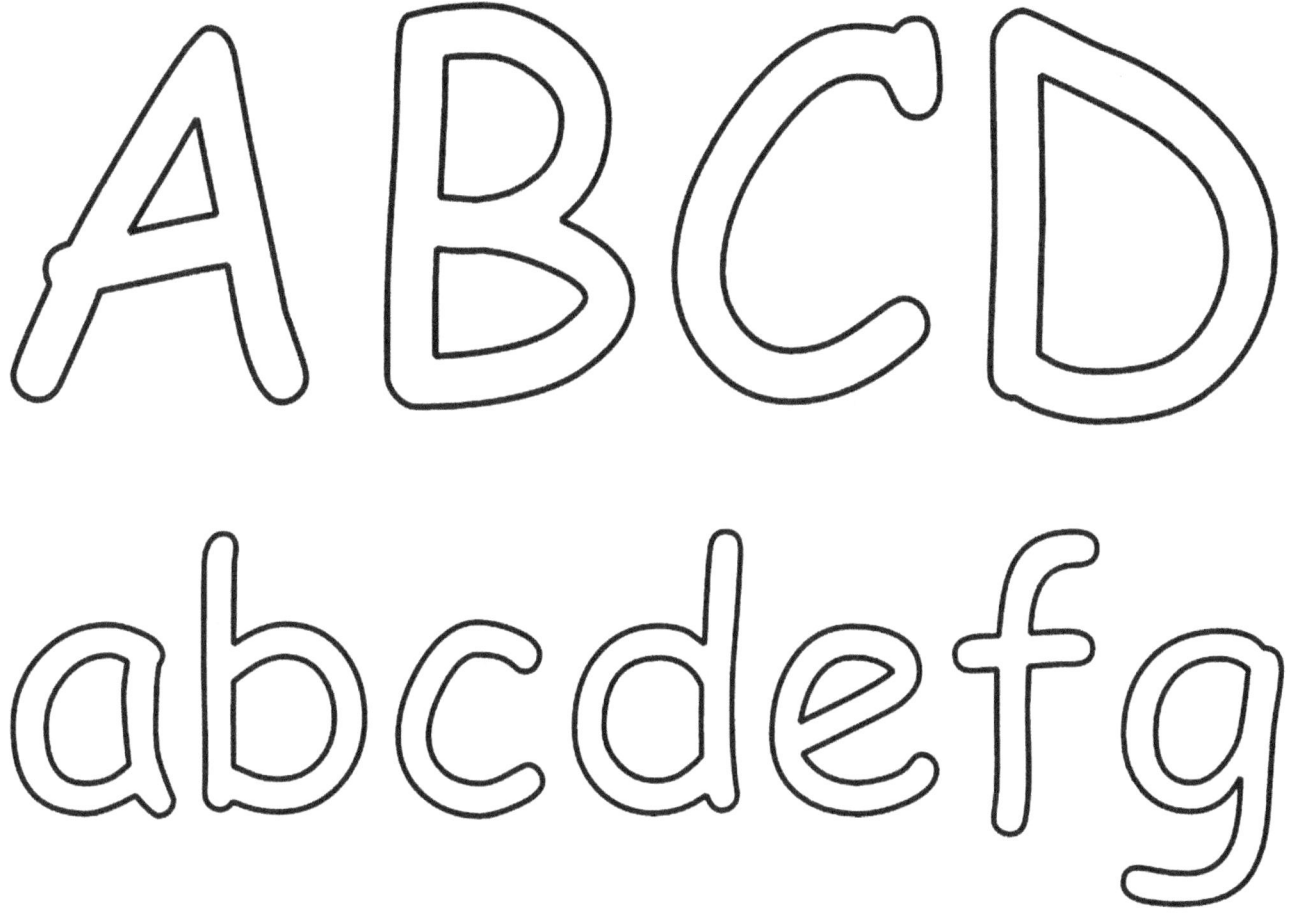

Comic Sans MS was developed for Microsoft in 1995. It is included with Microsoft Windows, and is often considered the most-hated typeface.

Cooper Black

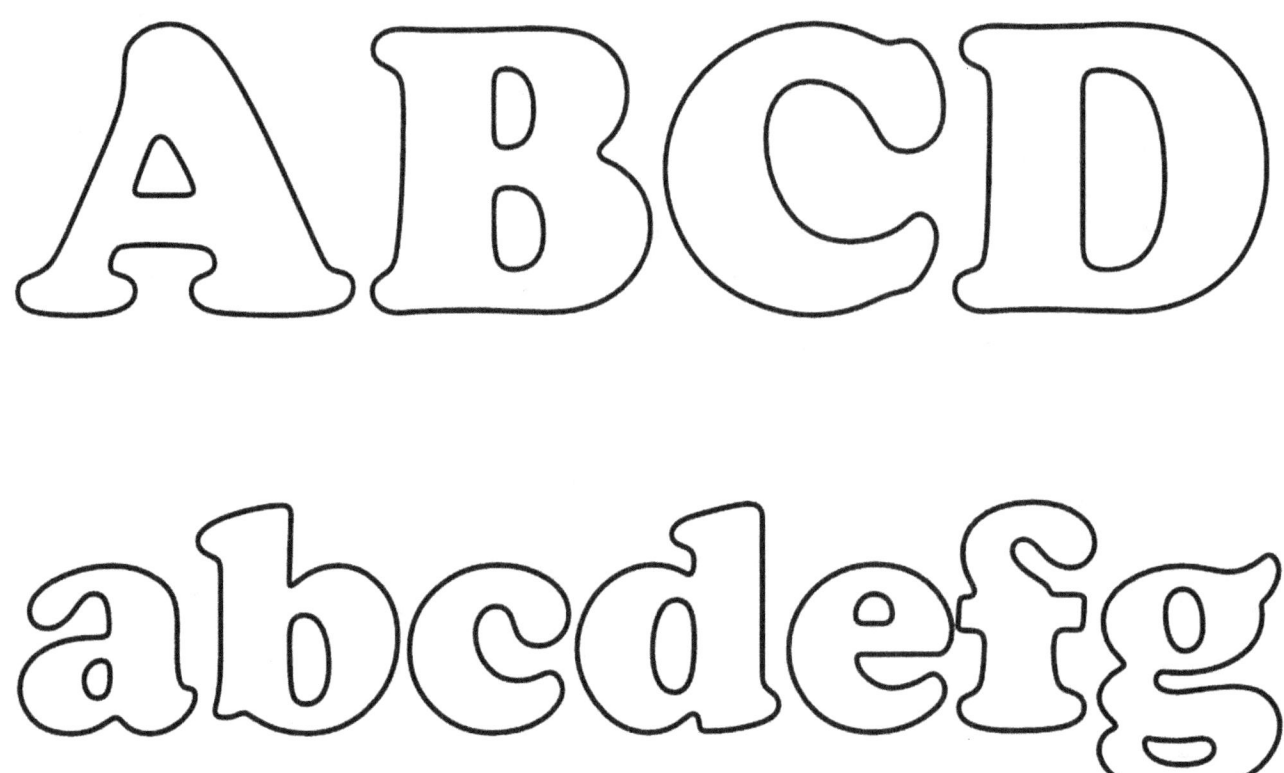

Cooper Black was designed by Oswald Bruce Cooper in 1921. It enjoyed a renaissance in the 1970s, and is still widely used in advertising.

Tootsie Roll wrappers and the Beach Boys'
Pet Sounds both feature Cooper Black.

Frankfurter

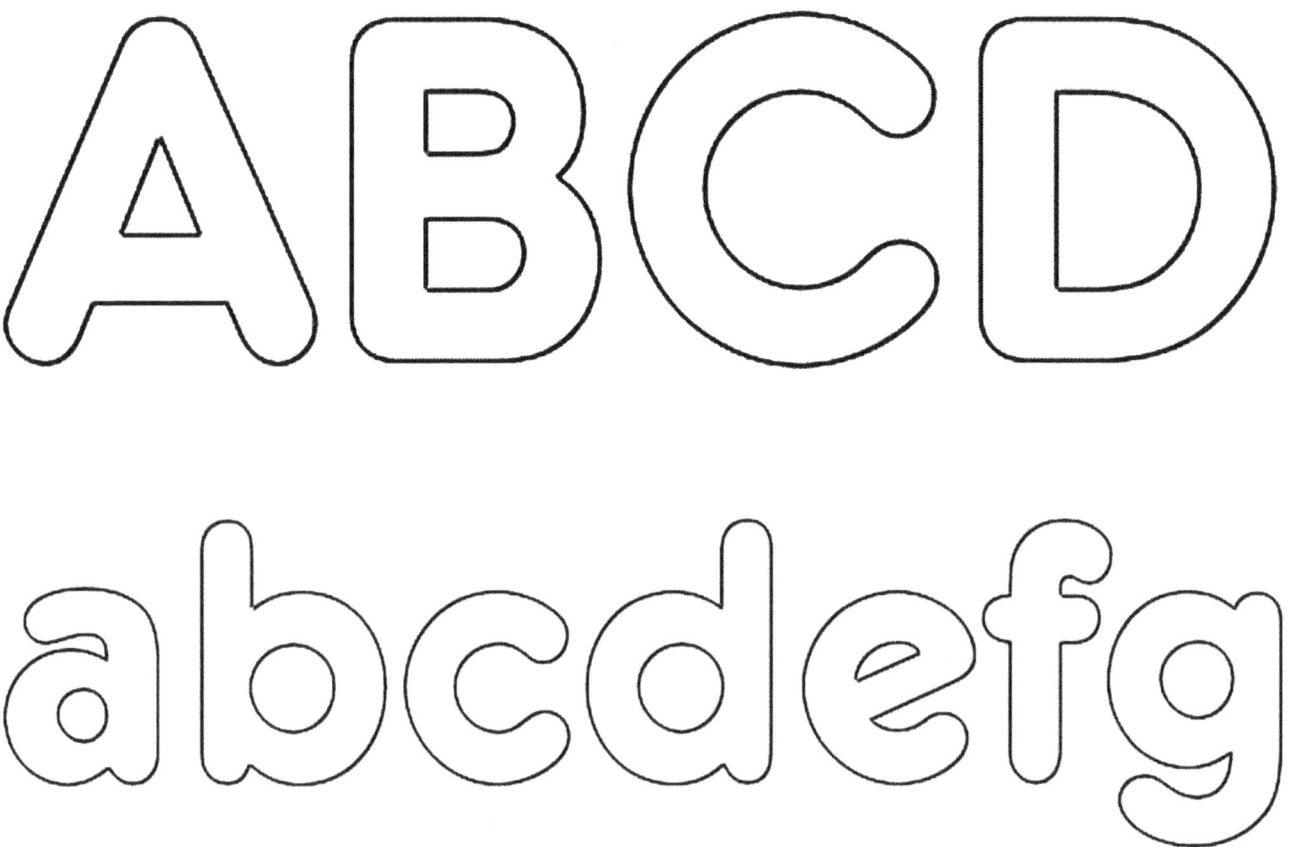

Frankfurter was designed by Nick Belshaw and Alan Meeks in the late 1970s.

Frankfurter is familiar to many because
of its use in the Dunkin' Donuts logo.

Futura

Futura was designed by Paul Renner in 1927, and is commonly associated with the Bauhaus design style.

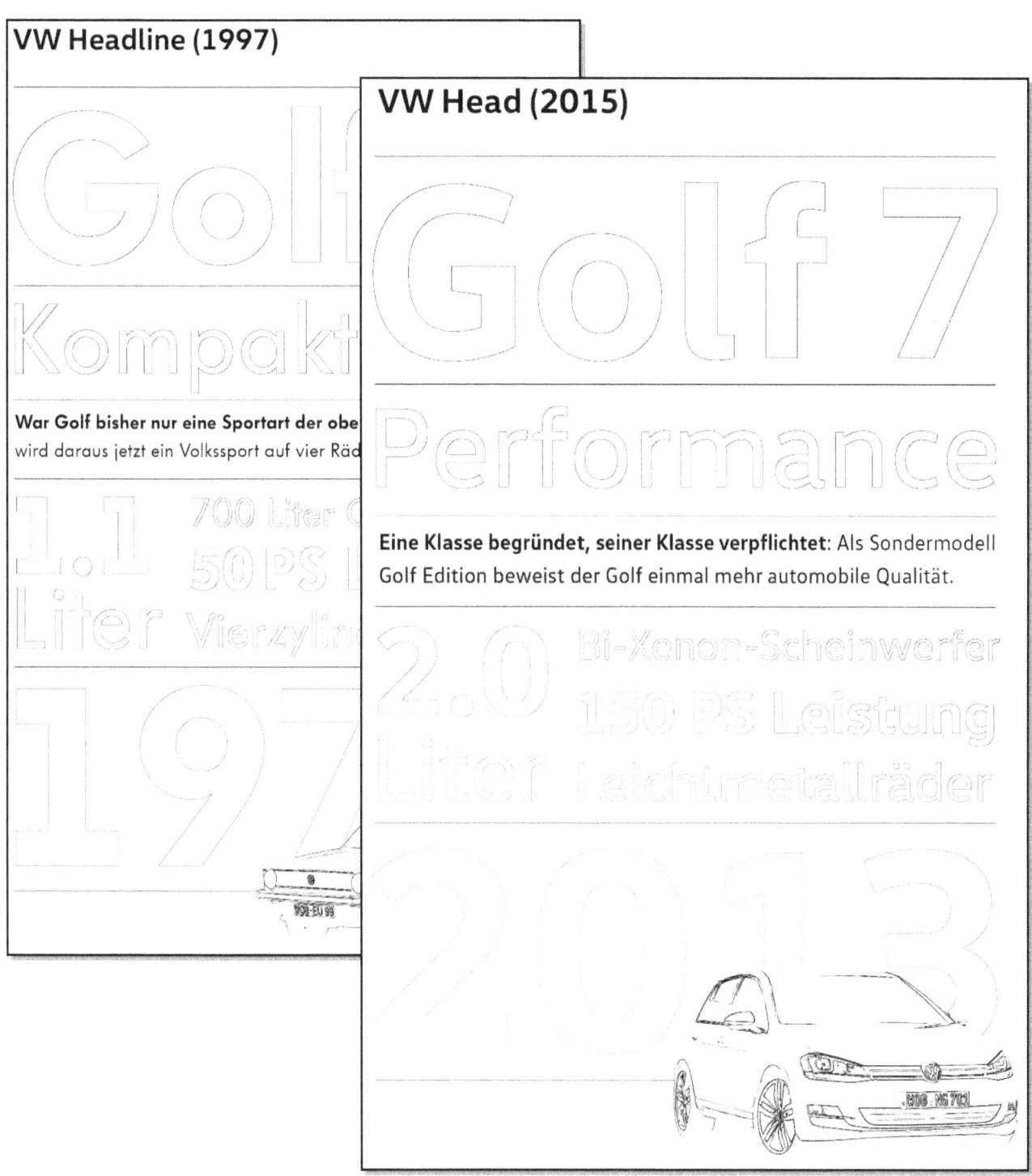

In 2015 Volkswagen announced that it was dropping its Futura variant in favor of a custom typeface by MetaDesign.

Garamond

ABCD

abcdefg

Garamond was designed in the 16th century by French engraver Claude Garamont.

EST. 1892

Abercrombie & Fitch

NEW YORK

The Abercrombie & Fitch logo uses
Garamond and Helvetica.

Gill Sans

Gill Sans was designed by Eric Gill in 1926. It was used by British Railways for many years and remains in wide usage today, especially in the United Kingdom.

BBC adopted Gill Sans in 1997.

Helvetica

Helvetica was developed in 1957 by Max Miedinger and Eduard Hoffmann. It is one of the most popular typefaces in the world.

Helvetica, seen here in the American Apparel logo, is widely used in advertising.

Impact

Impact was designed by Geoffrey Lee in 1965. Its current popularity likely results from its inclusion in Microsoft Windows.

Impact is commonly used in Internet memes, possibly because it stands out well when superimposed over a photograph.

Motter Tektura

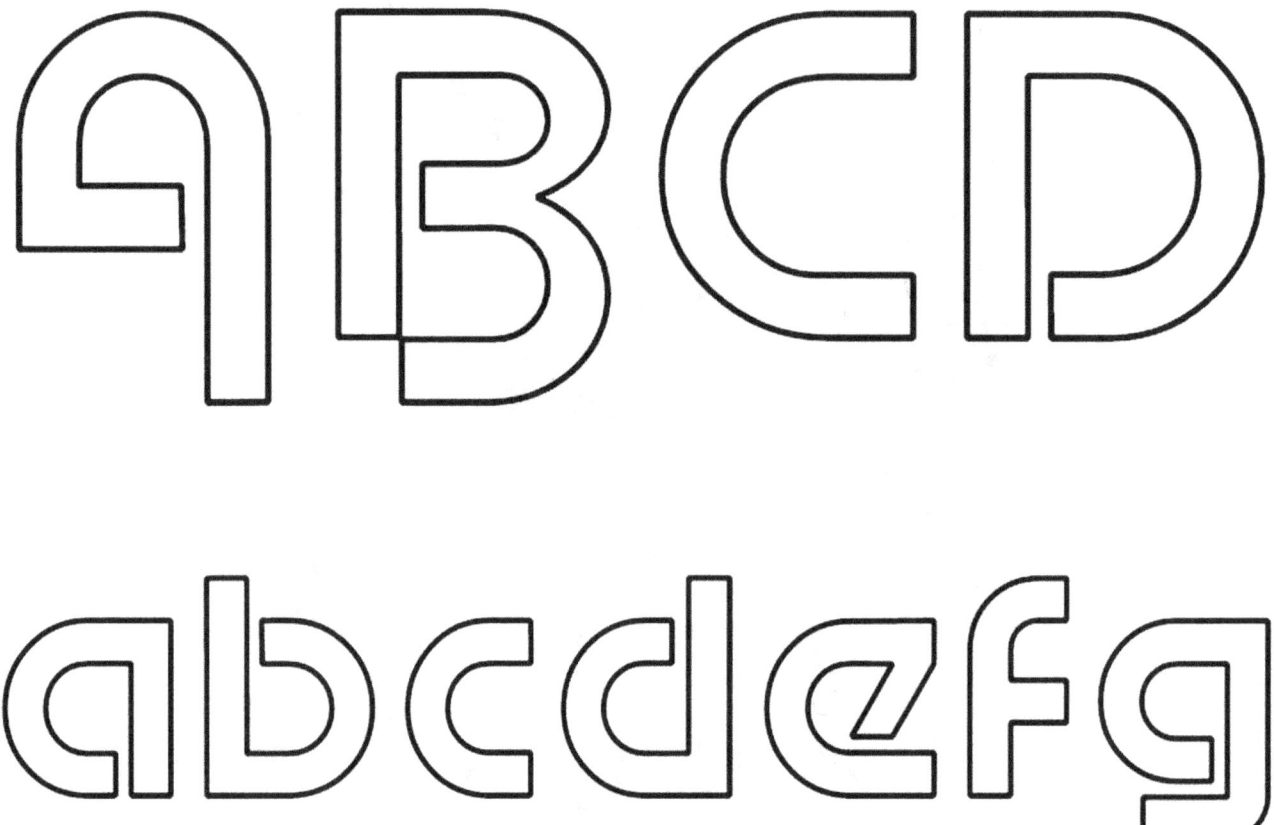

Motter Tektura was designed by Othmar Motter in 1975.

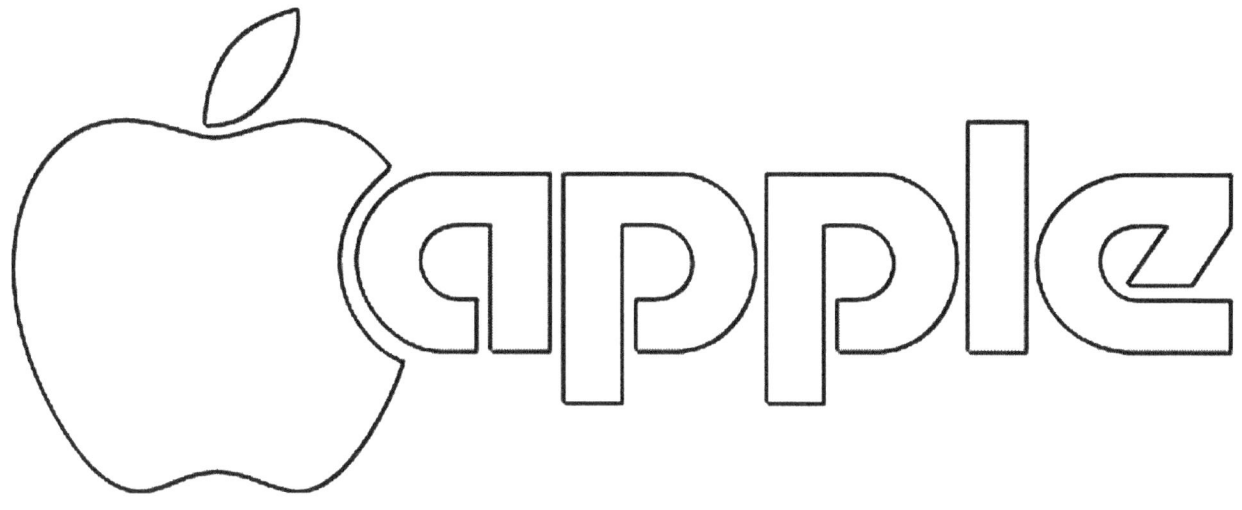

Apple Computer and Reebok both used
Motter Tektura in their former logos.

Myriad

Myriad was designed by Robert Slimbach and Carol Twombly for Adobe. It replaced Apple Garamond as Apple's corporate typeface in 2002.

News Gothic

Designed by Morris Fuller Benton, News Gothic was released in 1908.

Optima

Optima was designed by Hermann Zapf in the early 1950s. Zapf also designed Palatino and many other typefaces.

John McCain's 2008 presidential campaign
used the Optima typeface.

Papyrus

Papyrus was created by Chris Costello in 1982. Like Comic Sans, Papyrus is the subject of frequent derision.

The 2009 movie *Avatar* inexplicably chose Papyrus for promotional materials and even its subtitles.

Peignot

Peignot was designed by A. M. Cassandre in 1937. In place of
traditional lower case letters, it incorporates a mix of lower case
and small capital letters.

Several television shows have used Peignot for titles, beginning with *The Mary Tyler Moore Show* in the 1970s.

Perpetua

Perpetua was designed by Eric Gill for Monotype, which released it in 1929.

Souvenir

Morris Fuller Benton designed Souvenir in 1914. It was widely used in the 1970s but its popularity has faded in recent years.

Stencil

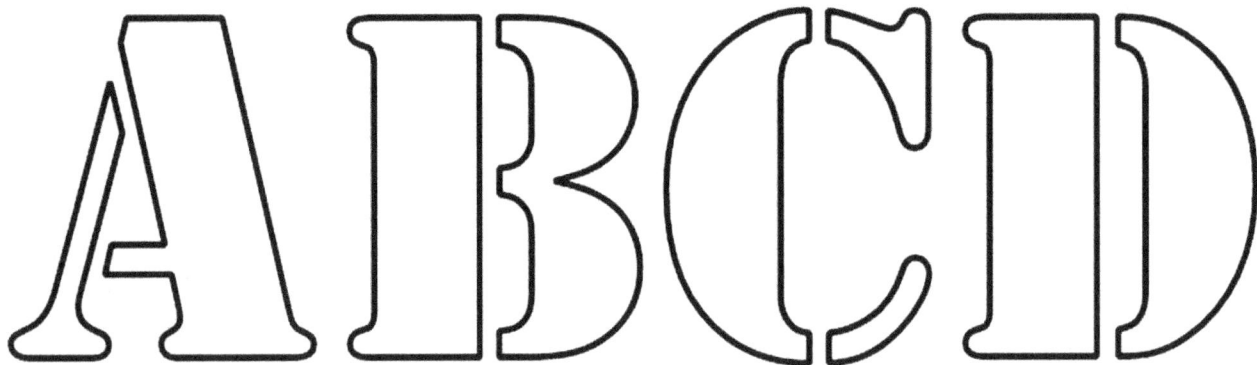

Stencil typefaces appeared in the late 1930s, generally with only upper case letters.

Stencil is used in The Home Depot's logo.

Times New Roman

ABCD

abcdefg

Times New Roman was commissioned by *The Times* (U.K.) in 1931, and was designed by Victor Lardent for Monotype. It is included with Microsoft Windows, and is among the most widely used typefaces.

Twentieth Century

Twentieth Century was designed by Sol Hess in 1937 as a competitor to Futura. The text of this book is set in Twentieth Century.

Verdana

Verdana was designed by Matthew Carter for Microsoft. It is intended for online use rather than print, being legible even at small sizes on low-resolution displays.

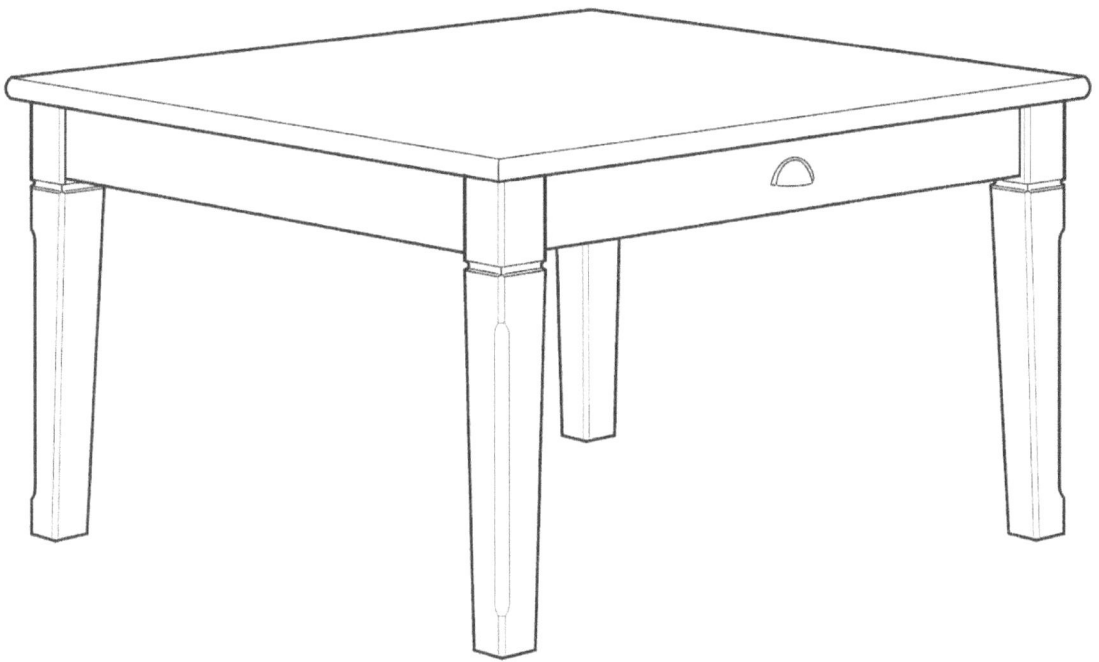

Coffee table

MARKÖR

90x90x52 cm
dark brown

► 2 drawers in the table underframe, suitable for storing remote controls, etc.

► Solid wood; gives a natural feel.

Coffee table

MARKÖR

90x90x52 cm
dark brown

► 2 drawers in the table underframe, suitable for storing remote controls, etc.

► Solid wood; gives a natural feel.

In 2009 IKEA replaced its custom version of Futura with the more widely available Verdana.